SIGNS
OF LIFE

KPT PUBLISHING

SIGNS OF LIFE

Copyright © 2018 KPT Publishing

Published by KPT Publishing
Minneapolis, Minnesota 55406
www.KPTPublishing.com

ISBN 978-1-944833-32-9

Design and production by Koechel Peterson and Associates, Minneapolis, Minnesota

All rights reserved. No part of this publication may be reproduced, stored in a retrieval system, or transmitted in any form or by any means—electronic, mechanical, digital, photocopy, recording, or any other—except for brief quotations in printed reviews, without the prior permission of the publishers.

First printing March 2018

10 9 8 7 6 5 4 3 2 1

Printed in the United States of America

SIGNS
OF LIFE

PREPARE YOURSELF

Please
CHECK UNDER
YOUR CAR
Before driving away

BEWARE OF DOGS

STRICTLY NON-VEGETARIAN

PLEASE UNLOAD GUN

AND

REMOVE SKI MASK

BEFORE ENTERING

PLEASE BE SAFE.

**Do not stand, sit, climb or lean on fences.
If you fall, animals could eat you and that might make them sick.
Thank you.**

UNLESS YOUR DOG CAN DO THIS...

PLEASE BE RESPONSIBLE AND CLEAN UP AFTER THEM

 REP... 788-4000
99/028

WOOD BUFFALO

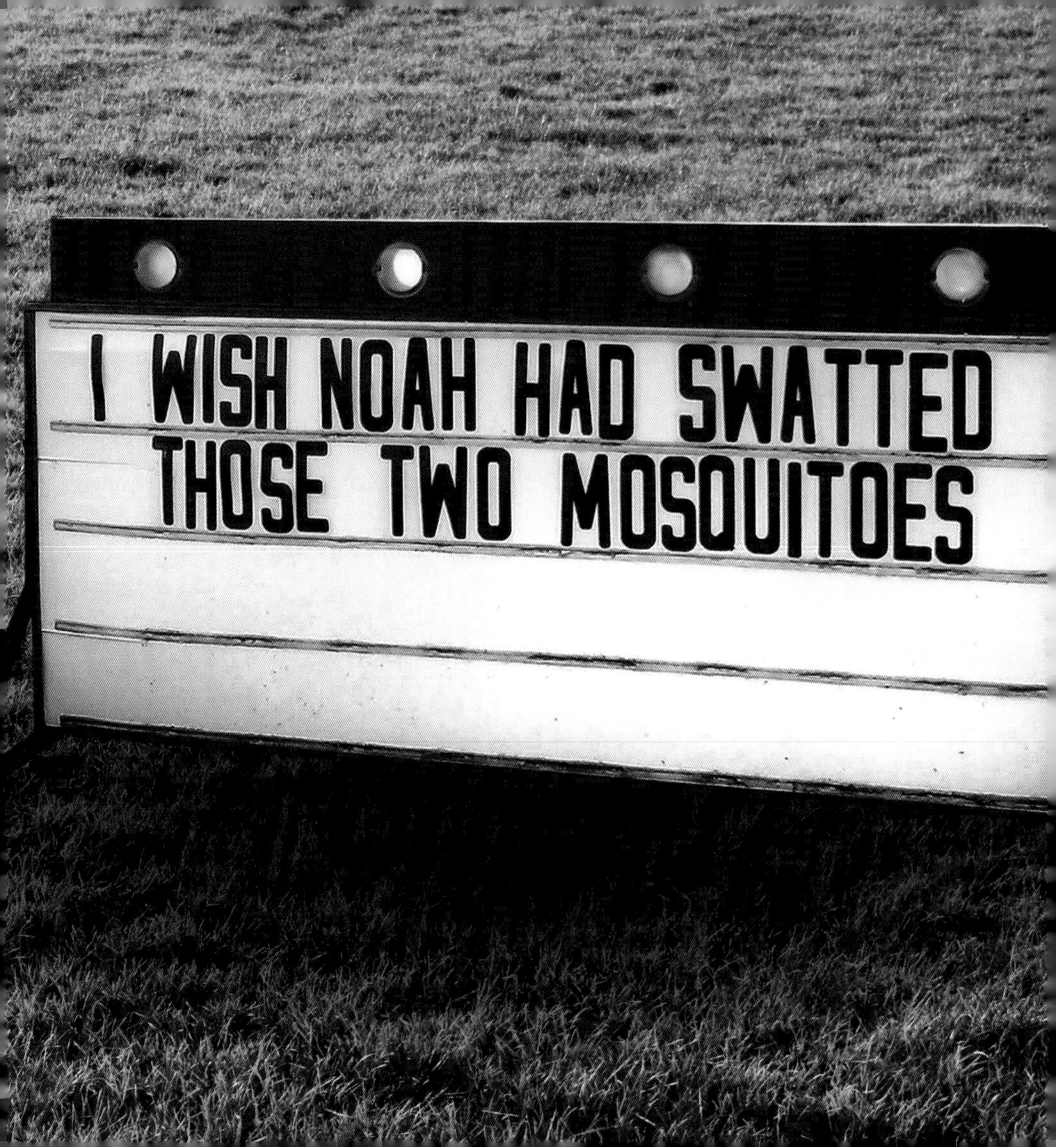
I WISH NOAH HAD SWATTED
THOSE TWO MOSQUITOES

Las Vegas is a city of glitz and bright lights, and just about everywhere you look you can find neon lights blazing. There are actually over 15,000 miles of neon tubing in the city. The glowing electric signs are so much a part of Vegas that there is a museum dedicated to it: the Neon Museum.

Wallaby's
LIQUOR
WAREHOUSE

IF ITS IN STOCK
WE VE GOT IT

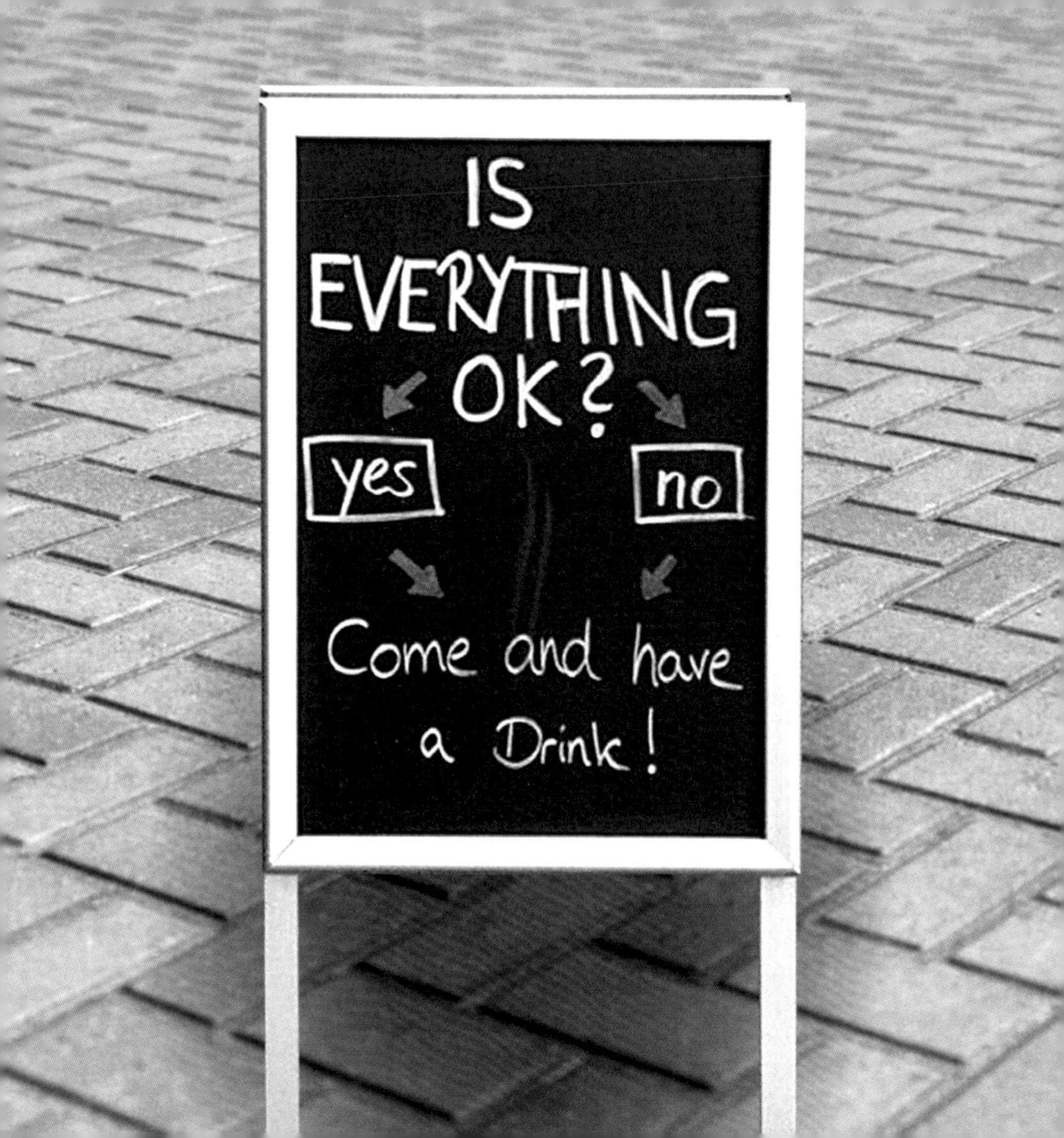
IS
EVERYTHING
OK?
yes
no
Come and have
a Drink!

PROBABLY THE BEST BEER IN THE WORLD

HUNGRY?
we will FEED YOU
THIRSTY?
we will get you DRUNK
LONELY?
WE WILL GET YOU DRUNK

Wall Street is often used as a term to refer to the financial part of New York. However, although New York's financial district is quite large, Wall Street itself is a street that runs for 8 blocks from Broadway to South Street in the financial district of New York and is just under half a mile long.

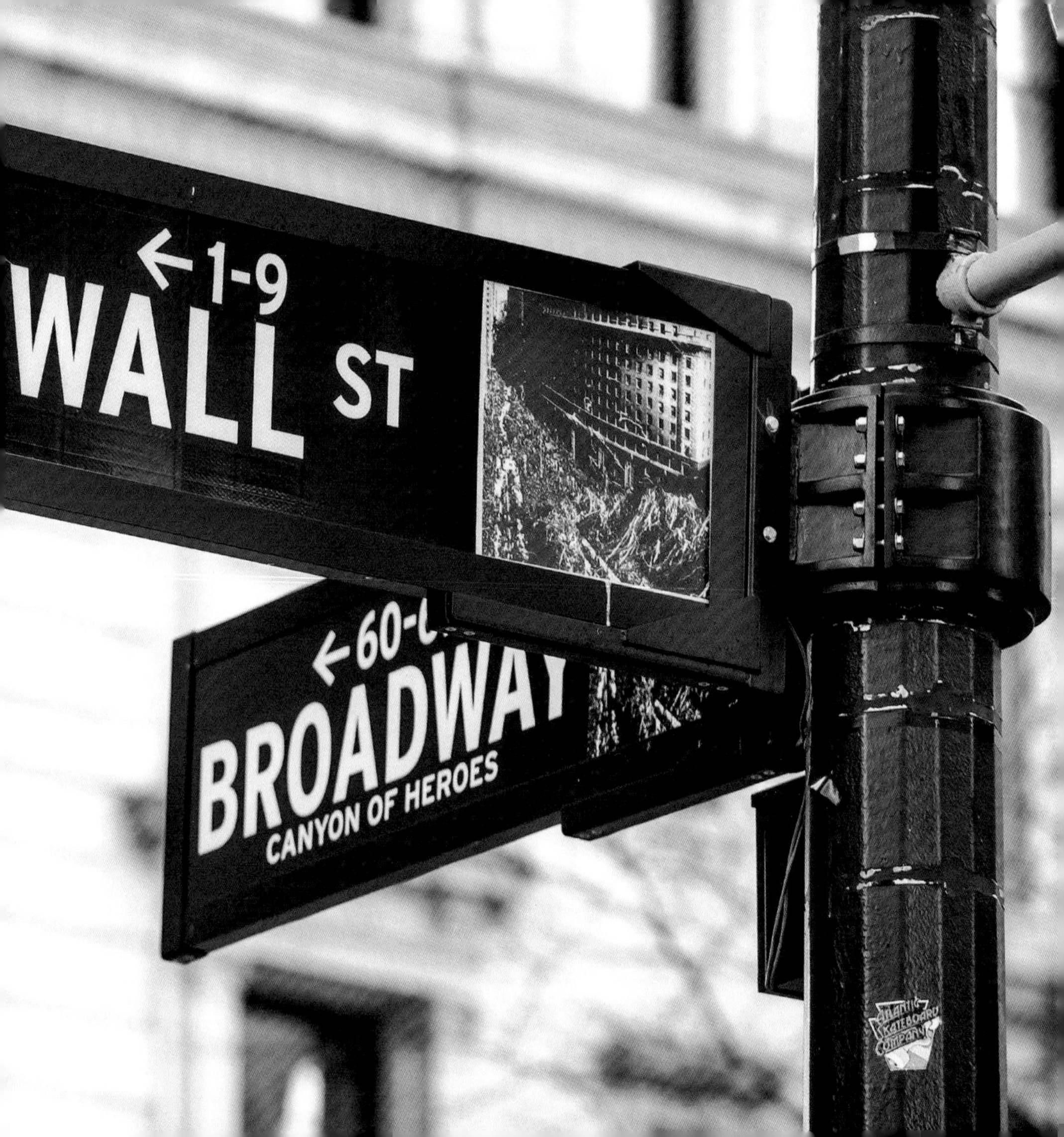
←1-9
WALL ST
BROADWAY
CANYON OF HEROES

CHURCH PARKING ONLY
Violators will be Baptized

THIS IS A CH CH.

WHAT'S MISSING?
U R

SUNDAY WORSHIP 7:45am & 10:30am   CHURCH SCHOOL 9:00am

I WAS ADDICTED TO
THE HOKEY POKEY
BUT I TURNED
MYSELF AROUND
BAN PRE-SHREDDED
CHEESE
MAKE AMERICA
GRATE AGAIN

24 HOUR EMERGENCY SERVICES
DINOSAURS NEVER
WENT TO THE VET
LOOK WHAT HAPPENED

To advertise the Hollywoodland development, the sign was composed of 13 letters that spelled out the development's name: "HOLLYWOODLAND." The last four letters of the sign wouldn't be dropped until 1949.

AmeriStop
Food Mart
OUR BOSS SAID
TO CHANGE THE
STUPID SIGN
SO WE DID

PAY TOILET
13¢

YOU ARE NOT
PERMITTED TO
SHARE OR
CRAWL UNDER
THESE STALLS

DO NOT ENTER
ENTRANCE ONLY

Route 66 starts in Chicago, Ilinois and ends in Santa Monica, California.

No Skinny DIPPING BEFORE 6 PM

24 HOUR VIDEO SURVEILLANCE

Blame the guy
who kept
pooping here.

The famous ivy in the outfield of Wrigley Field was planted by former Chicago White Sox owner Bill Veeck in 1937. Veeck, the son of former Cubs president Bill Veeck, Sr., would later own the Cleveland Indians, St. Louis Browns, and the Chicago White Sox. Veeck is also credited with the modernization of the concessions, as well as overseeing the 1937 bleacher and scoreboard construction. That said, the ivy, while planted by Veeck, was the brainchild of P. K. Wrigley, then owner of the club.

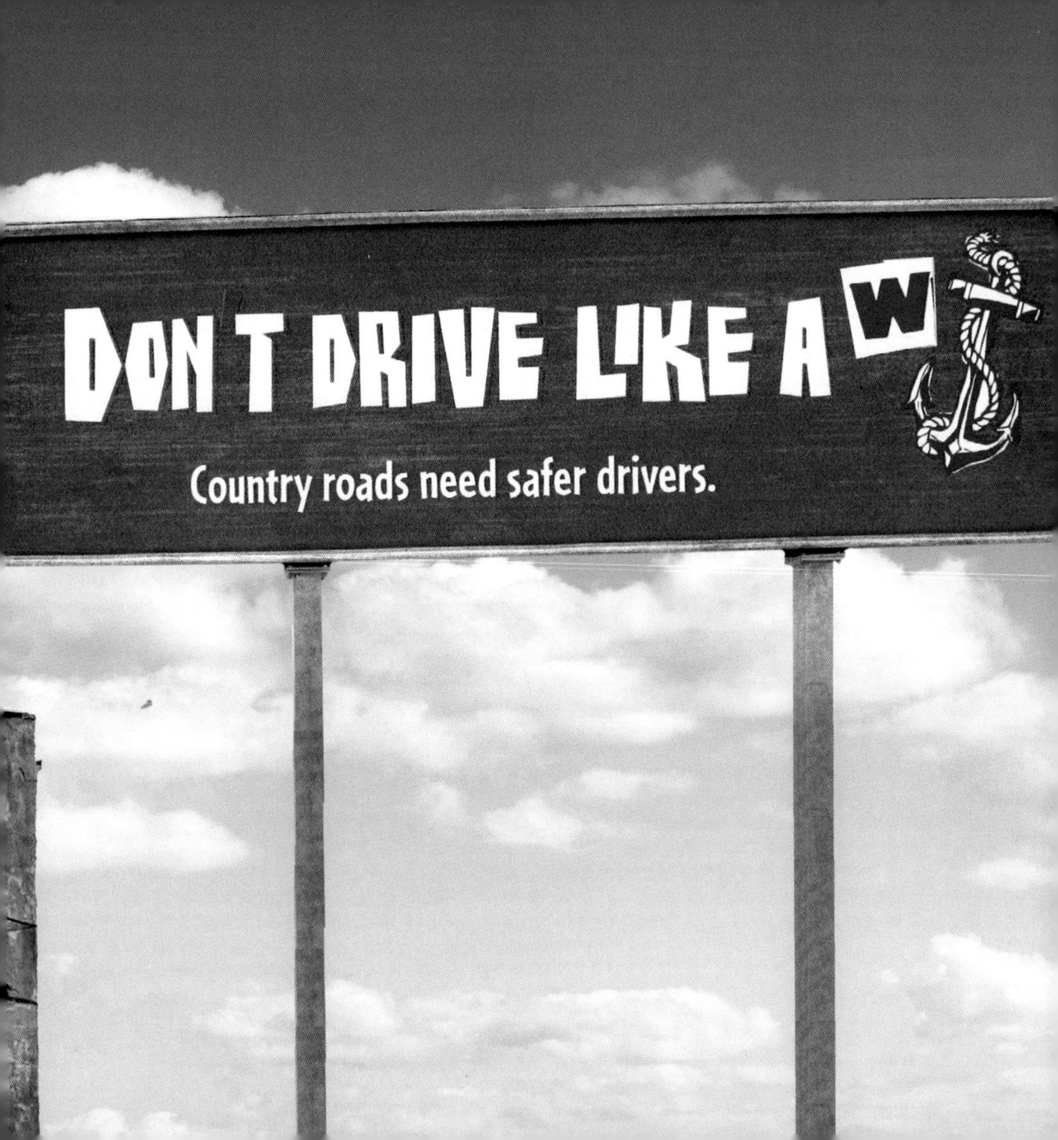
DON'T DRIVE LIKE A W
Country roads need safer drivers.

Forty-two bridges connect Key West to the mainland. The Overseas Highway is one of the most beautiful drives in the country. Completed in 1938, it connects a string of keys and coral rock with 113 miles of concrete roadway. The aptly named Seven Mile Bridge is the longest and most scenic.

THE CONCH REPUBLIC

90 Miles to CUBA

SOUTHERNMOST

POINT

CONTINENTAL U.S.A.

KEY WEST, FL
Home of the Sunset

One of the first passengers
on the Central Line, of the
London Underground, was
Mark Twain, in 1900.

CHANGING THE TOILET PAPER WILL NOT CAUSE BRAIN DAMAGE

TOILET

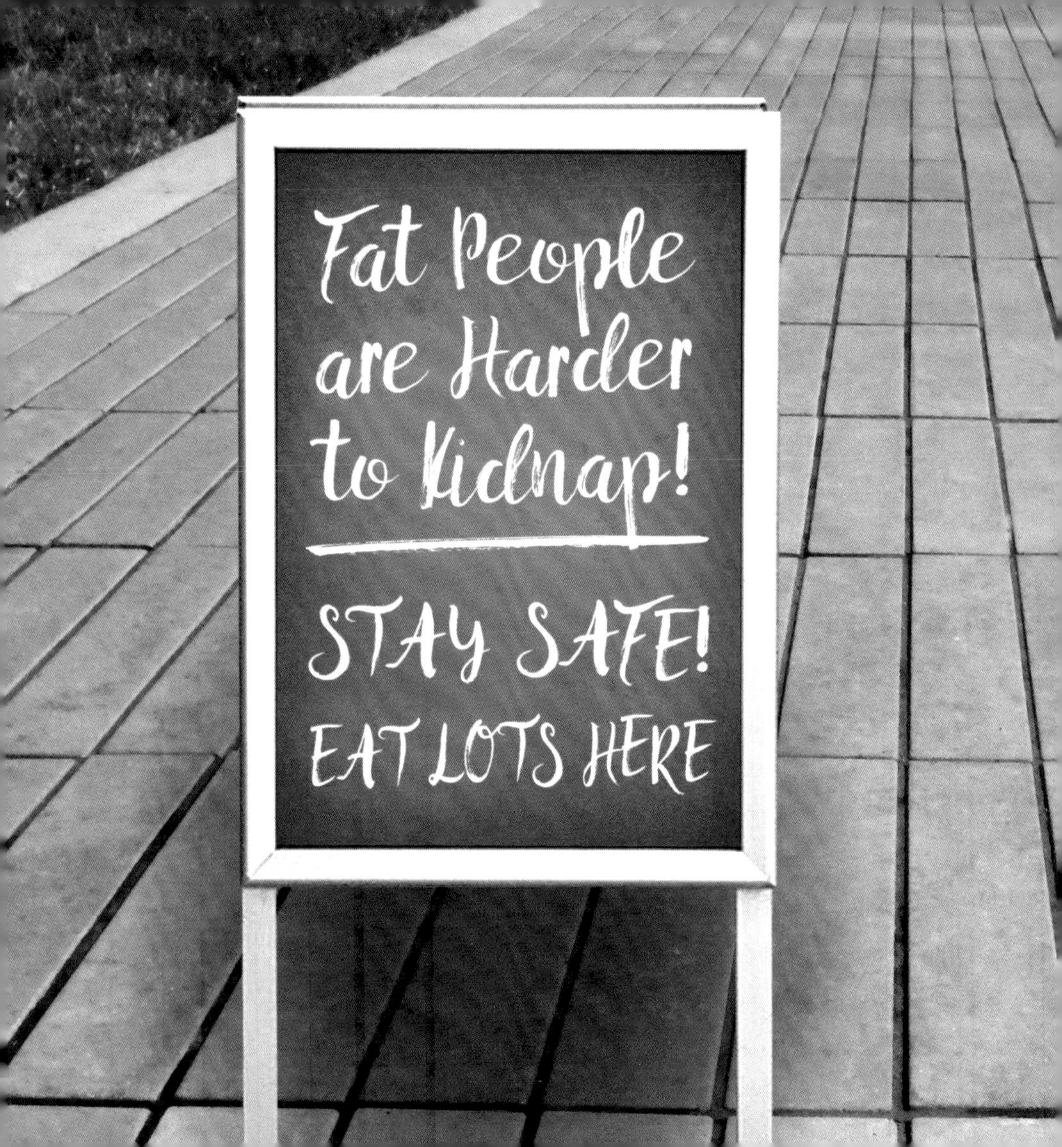
Fat People
are Harder
to Kidnap!
STAY SAFE!
EAT LOTS HERE

the

NAKED

truth about our

WAITRESSES

is they only

FLIRT

WITH YOU

to get better tips

Beverly Hills is the only city to boast:
no hospital, no cemetery, no billboards, and
no telephone or power lines. In 1930, horses
were banned by the city of Beverly Hills!

Ask me about my attention deficit disorder or my dog or pie. I have a bike, do you like ham? I like your shoes. Hi. What's your name?

FREE
BEER
TOMORROW

NOTICE!
IF YOU'RE DRINKING TO FORGET,
PLEASE
PAY IN ADVANCE

Trust me, you can dance.
— beer

For the simple Hard Rock logo, they enlisted Alan Aldridge to create their brand emblem, which was inspired by an old Chevrolet hood ornament. Aldridge was a bonafide celebrity artist who did a lot of work with The Beatles, Elton John, a slew of trippy Penguin book covers, among other stuff.

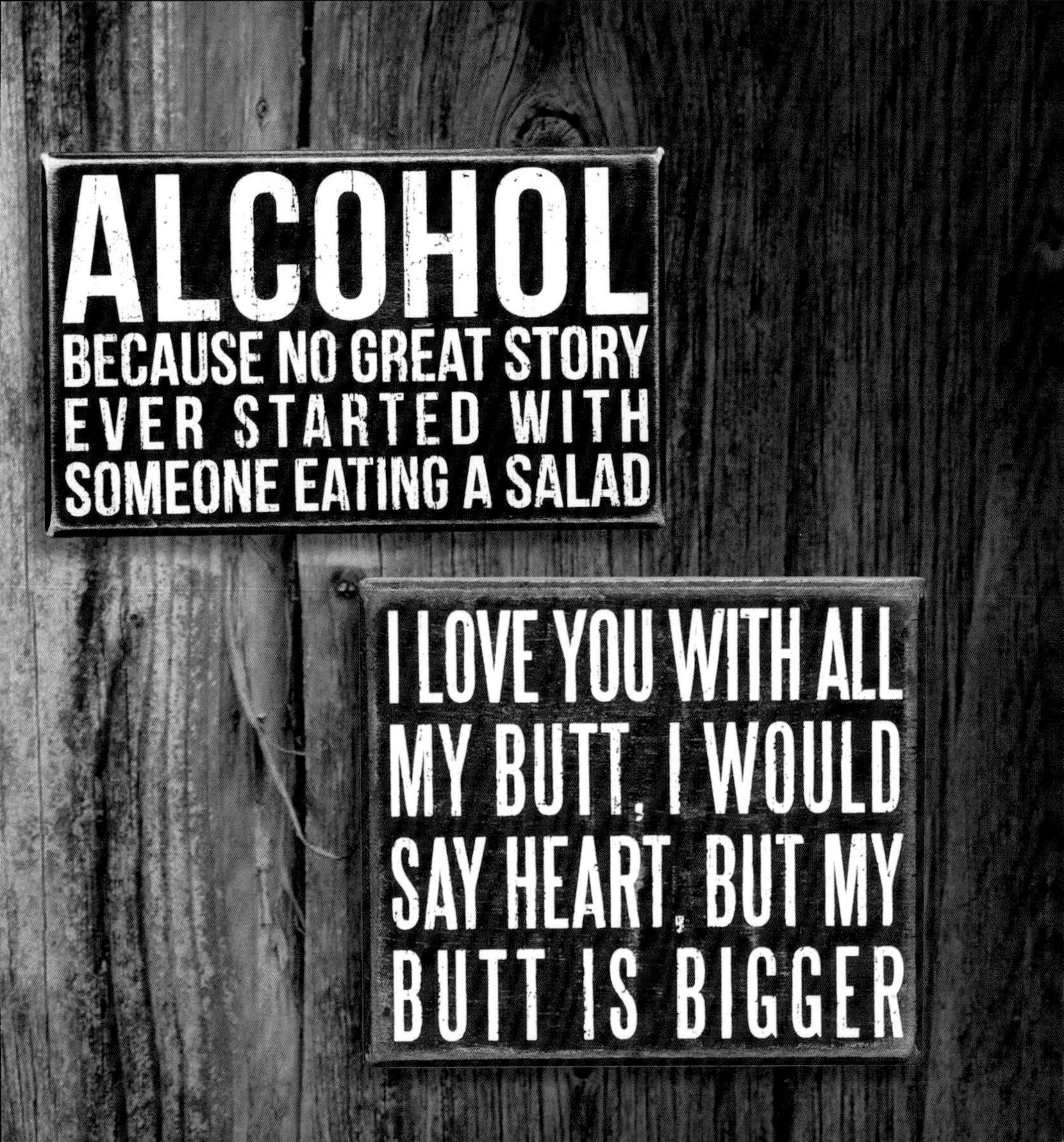

ALCOHOL
BECAUSE NO GREAT STORY
EVER STARTED WITH
SOMEONE EATING A SALAD

I LOVE YOU WITH ALL
MY BUTT, I WOULD
SAY HEART, BUT MY
BUTT IS BIGGER

PUT YOUR
LAUNDRY
AWAY, OR I'LL
PUNCH
YOU IN THE
FACE.
LOVE,
Mom
I'M NOT
WEIRD
I'M
LIMITED
EDITION

MARRIAGE IS LIKE A DECK OF CARDS

IN THE BEGINNING ALL YOU NEED
IS TWO HEARTS AND A DIAMOND.
IN THE END YOU WISH YOU HAD
A CLUB AND A SPADE.

CAUTION

DO NOT
DRINK WATER

FISH CRAP IN IT

Thousands of kangaroos are hit by cars and killed each year, and it is such a prevalent danger that you'll see the front of many Australian cars equipped with a bull 'roo bar as a result.